Charlie,

from Lana Yeshua

one Student to another

W xxx Time

Snow and Rumors of

Snow

– Readings from the Isle Top –

Timo Antero Raunela

ISBN # 9798843017491

Cover images and photography by Timo Antero Raunela.

Author can be contacted at:

timo.raunela@gmail.com

See also Instagram account: 'Sage_Of_HolyIsle'

Warm thanks to Holy Isle community for all those send-off and Ceilidh evening parties. Many of the poems in this collection had their first readings during these festivities.

Special thanks for Anne, Rose, Luke, Kate, Sandra, Vicki, Helen, Anthony and Howard for their support and inspiring words.

I am also very much indebted to Helen for her superb proof-reading skills.

Contents

II Eskhaton   55

Poem Kata

Dedicated to 17th Gyalwang Karmapa, Ogyen Trinley Dorje

To be ready to encounter
Language in its unravelling,
The sentences in their
Stitchless ends...

To witness it appear,
The invisible guest
Caught in the weaving
Of words...

To address it
To speak
Its mind in silence...

To shed light
In the white light of
Its spaciousness...

Coach yourself
For that special day,
Present forever there.

Speak for
The non-conceptual,
Be its keeper and its guard.

Like a child's drawing for its Mum,
Give an offering to your beloved,
The one who waits
For us all.

Because for the Buddhas
To know your way around poetry
Is always
A great gift.

I On Far-Offs and Close-Bys

Road Movie

I

It wasn't that much that we were, what people name: 'in love'. There were just so many lines coinciding in our road map palm readings.

Was it your country or mine? As we drove past unfamiliar terrain at night fall, not much could be ascertained. With stone walls of sleep closing in on us and being constantly bombarded by rainy headlights, our eyes missed a lot.

We exchanged childhood traumas like mobile numbers, dumbfounded by the alikeness in code. How you had become the man you were and how I somehow made it here, just by us both dialling a random set of digits causing our longitudes and latitudes to merge?

There was also an attempt to try to ensure our directions would not be based on the eye-perspective. Instead of relying on the street view we stuck to the maps connecting A to B wherever we could. Turning folds around in our hands like they were pieces of a puzzle, with a picture full of gaps and scene changes reminiscent of dream sequences. It was like we managed to piece together something that made sense on the spot. Yet it all seemed nothing short of bonkers if thoroughly scrutinized.

II

The dusk turned into early evening. We realized it was no longer possible to continue driving without risking you falling asleep, so we decided to pull in at the nearest motel. I was initially suspicious of our room having a water bed, worried that it might bring ruptures and leaks to our dreams, but ended up being rather care-free about it.

Chuckling about the plot twist we double dived into our bed. As the swell subsided alongside our racing hearts, we both fell silent. The rain was still there, but now its tin roof tap dancing was somewhat muffled. The car park and the opposite doors heaved back and forth like waves of deep blue glass. There were also irregular punctuations of wall sized TV-screens behind windows emitting soundless light show, which I for a moment mistook for lightning. Time slowed down.

After a while you took my hand to yours and joined our palms together. You then snapped your fingers, almost like trying to wake me up from a trance or hypnosis, but nothing happened. There was only a popping sound in my inner ear.

That was it, for the night at least. The oracle had neither spoken nor hidden his meaning, but instead given a sign. The reading offered no directions, only calling for intensified attention. Relieved by the fact that we now had nothing to find our bearings with, we fell asleep in each other's arms.

Ley Lines

The row of huts

following the line of

island's spine

to the distance;

a posture encircled with

magnetic fields

of the old.

Laying on your back

For years on end.

Exchanging rings of ore

and moss growing

in slow-mo time-lapse;

the wedding ceremony of

pasture and water.

The sun's yarn ball

of minute changes of axis,

power charged

with patterns

of less sleep,

radiates states of hypnosis

you cannot remember.

And who needs dreams

anyway

when one can watch

YouTube-videos

of guides in Ecuador

demonstrating *Coriolis Effect*

to groups of tourists.

Until it starts to lag

and traces back

its lost tracks

in renewed circles,

suspending and displacing

reason of a dream

so far away.

Focal Point

People with longer connection to Holy Isle claim the energy at the top of the island is so strong, that most people find it difficult to camp on Mullach Mor overnight. Some have tried, but they can't seem to get sleep while staying there.

I wish they had not told me that. Because now every time I think about it, a weirdly persistent image pops up in my head. This is a picture of Buddhas, Arhats and ordinary practitioners levitating on the top of Holy Isle Stupas. Yes, you got it right. Not on top of Mullach Mor, but on top of each of the Stupas. Some of the people are sitting cross-legged. Some levitators lay on their backs or on their sides. Some are asleep, some are awake.

What makes the image even more outrageous is the fact its style is similar to a particular political satire cartoon I saw once. In it a fakir lays on top of a single spike and one of the onlookers makes a wisecrack about it.

Meanwhile, I try not to mind the stern gazes of those awake and go on circumambulating it all, casting mantras with mala-rosary in my hand, wondering what they could become. Sleeping bags and Mullach Mor at night? Mixed band of meditators? The real fakir? A random newspaper page? Or maybe just a missed joke about nothing and everything?

At Midsummer Bonfire

Memorial from Hämeenkyrö, Finland

Starting to split into separate parties,
We strolled along towards the bathing beach.

Dogs and kids, childhood friends and villagers.
Some familiar faces and some new ones.

The shoreline alder canopy on the
Top of the forest road became denser,

And for a moment the night darkened to
August.
                    Then the clearing.

A freshly shortened circle of reed bed,
In the middle of which a big blazing flame

Basked in the spotlight, under gazes of
                    Eyes rubbed and cleared.

[15]

Sparks, as restless as children... Playing with embers
Glowing on sticks. Bouncing up and down

Adults getting tipsy. From the suction
Of the big flame back to the cars, or

Escaping mosquitos... Away and back,
Away and back... Upwards, to the whirling.

On the sides... In and out, and back to
Out of sight...

Inside the pyre non-flickering flames
All amassed. The dark and deep surrounding

The lit wicks of the candles, as still as
Peaty lakes of the region.
                    Will-o'-the-wisps,

The inklings of which only drunken senseless
And shamans gone into trance can have.

Worldling

1

At springtime I used to aim at things about you with a magnifying glass. Considering at this stage green gunge was still running from my nose, for my age I was focused. In my hands a piece of bark with contour of a lizard resting on it, turned into a crackling sphinx. A plastic bag was just another drifter out there in the wasteland. Through my hands this duckling changed into a kerosene smelling swan. Each sunny day was another fun adventure of turning something into ashes or seeing something as something. Like a god, I'd been given a permit to destroy and create. So I did.

2

I'd still want to   write you   down though,

                                   take notes.

But you   couldn't   care less.

General rule being   you refuse   to shine

                                   or to stay

                                   in focus

You just   squirt   in the corners

or

                    fade away

                                   from the scene

                                   all together.

You come in   and go out   like a cat:

                   in your own time.

3

You're basically dealing with someone a bit green,

who's totally over his head with the ways of the

world. Don't ask me about method, optics or:

'How to do the trick?' Depths that I know nothing

of. There's only obstinate and unpredictable love,

which nevertheless for some unfathomable reason

gives.

Halfway Hostel

I am your halfway hostel.
Deemed wanting you will never need me
Like the air you breathe.

Affront and eyesore of not pampering
Your ego; your personal space,
Your belongings, your precious comfort zone.

My friendship like a hard bed,
On which you lie sleepless half the night.
Unable to keep down your deranged demons.

Always ready to meet you halfway
So you can drop your keys of mixed feelings
With thanks or without them, while expecting neither.

Yet when you return home and discomfort is gone,
You are better off with than without
Some eerie glimpse of light you needed to see.

Fancies for Life

All the sailing yachts that anchored near Holy Isle
shore over the course of the year, with sounds of
distant chatter over the water, evening light reflecting
through lipstick stained plastic wine glasses and yacht
dinghies shamelessly trying to have it off with our jetty
like they were some kind of mating season bath ducks
of affluence; all those images were oddly alien, as if
the blurred surroundings from which they stood out,
were of unclear origin.

Did the things themselves dream then, or were the
images just apparitions? Or maybe the whole thing
was someone else's most cherished memory!?
Something they will keep to themselves the rest of their
lives and will only speak about on their death beads?
*'You remember that time when we anchored near
Arran, and spent the evening talking and swimming?
That for me was the happiest day of my life. After that
with us it started to get messy.'*

Never-Never Family

1

Some of us have it, some of us don't.
Somewhat unusual part of the family saga,
Initiated by some sad ending, which
Later yielded an odd offspring. Some kind of
Drama in which there was an abrupt
Divide of the two parties until
Remainder of either love or death.
This fruit of love will never be
Quite sure of whether it is actually
Living, or is it just a figment of
One possibility. And therefore always feels
Unaccounted for. A trauma which is
Not alleviated by the fact,
That it all now – when engaging with the
Known part of the family – is just a
Hush-hushed parallel world,
Never unfolding fully to the
Experiences we call reality.

There could also be
Eerie images from far-away places,
Bothersome like eyes staring at you from
Behind the curtains. All of it like
Something left hanging in the air, like
A still from a film you've never seen, or an
Unfinished business of a former life with a
Blank business card.

2
You are drawn to them of course, these
Non-nameable family members. And why
Wouldn't you be? Born out of one body
Of Buddha, in which every being is
Your mother, father and brothers.

It's an alluring daydream;
That your ache of not fitting in would have a
Counter-balance. Lost oracles of the family
Showing up to explain this or that
Uncanny out of character trait in you
That makes you uneasy. Offering an
Explanation that would put your mind at rest.

But that of course is a fairy tale.
Even Buddhas have to deal with something
Inaccessible. Maybe it is some kind of
Residue of ignorance, which you just have to
Allow to do its part? Allow it to
Devour those conceptual projections like
Kronos ate his children. A brutal process in which
The birth of remembering is cancelled.
After that it's just getting ready for
The opening scene, which in
All likelihood will be shot at some
Operating theatre in Finland.
A scene of neither knowing nor sharing;
A holy family in which no-one knows
Each other's names captured in
Unfocused images.

Snow and Rumours of Snow

I
A hill
Half hidden
In the mist,

With its steel blue
Quickly changing
Into snow clouds.

Then a sudden shower
Of sleet diving
Into wet black rocks,

Like a flock of
Shooting gannets
Piercing the surface,

And for few magical seconds
The dream world of underneath
Envelopes us;

A mirror like place
In which only rumours of snow
Are echoed.

II
Up on the hilltops
Mist is almost gone.

The pathways now whitened
Like veins of clarity

Slowly gathering
For greater crossings.

You close your eyes
And map the 'snowscape'.

Its ether at once
Wide scale and intimate

And its white cold radiating
From ground below;

Our dreams' cornerstones
Firmly buried

Inside snow's
Hearsay underworld.

III
They say all pathways
Lead to love,
But we are unsure
Where ours is heading.

Instead we surrender
To the gentle seduction
Of not knowing
Where we're at,

Almost like
Being bewildered,
But in a way
That is enticing.

You then lock

Your eyelids

To half closed position

And notice

As the snow beneath our feet

Starts to pull us

Towards something

Drowsy below.

Looking-Glass

I thought I'd just take a short nap.
But the moment I dozed off,
I was startled by a dream.

I saw a hawk of
Some sort, jumping about by
What looked like a farm gate.

Raking frantically
Through the dead spring grass.
And then it saw me.

I guess it wasn't that alarmed
By me, because It didn't
Fly away immediately.

It was the distraction
That did it.
It lost its prey.

The way it looked
At me before it took off, was
Impenetrable but telling.

I reckon it was
My dream seeing
Me with hawk's eyes;

Ones seeing through
Everything, even with
Just one blink.

Strict in its ways with
Retina reflections, it does not
Look kindly at distractions.

On Things

How things show forth, has none of the markings of
an empty kingly seat. Rather, theirs are the motifs
of 'obscure' and 'suggestive'. For example just
now the rain declared its start on the roof. And
there is an accelerating car with powerful engine
wanting attention somewhere on the other side of
the bay. And someone is quietly closing the gate.
They stand out in time as things you wonder about.
You start from that. You don't bind yourself to a
stance you will not hold. That it's just coinciding
events. Or that they by themselves somehow
already are poetry; that in there a hidden lyre
plays to lure us to the core of things. For sure there
is density there, some sort of texture, like a row of
combined notes, written with such small
handwriting you have to play them by ear.

Wordless, like the eerie humming of the dead, its meaning is lost to mankind. Yet each day scribes yet another slightly different cryptic line, so that, I like Penelope, can patiently weave and unravel their workings, cunningly buying time that lets them spring forth over and over again, while all along picking threads for my spinnings and weavings. Some things coloured, some things of the old, some things stolen or some things of my own. Whatever the combination of the outcome, it always has to be enough to keep the lovers of words guessing.

Modern Abandon

There is an aching reason yearning to be heard
at the furthest recesses of the tacit. Someone
half-whispers the word 'police brutality' – as if
wanting to make sure no-one feels awkward. And
when things are at their normal place, there is a
tinge of a feeling of everything being out of
hand. Yet you convinced yourself it all is as it
should be.

Little birds Morse-code your windows with their
beaks, mindlessly reporting the chaos out there.
Some emergency vehicle going by with racket
and flashing blue lights upsets your TV-on sofa
sleep; awakening as rude as melting hail on
summer lawn. You feel tired; you've worked hard.
You've earned this soothing space.

On States of Mind

I

There is no such a thing as a state of mind,

Because if such a state existed,

Its leader would immediately be killed.

His death followed by a fast paced succession of

Coup d'états, revolutions and counter revolutions.

Each demon army claiming to regain the land
And dividing it justly.

Troops criss-crossing the country

And with each conflict ensuing chaos increasing.

Towns and villages war-zoned,

Pillaged and razed to the ground.

Leaving in the end only a heap of ashes of conditions

Impossible for peaceful human existence;

A heap of misery akin murderers and rapists we are.

II

Is there anything you can do?

Or rather, anything you can

Avoid doing?

Leave the state!

Leave the state of your mind!

Leave it as it is!

Place no shock value

In its actions of

'Shock and awe'.

Displaced and borderless,

Welcome every encounter

As something to dwell on.

Appreciate also all things

Inconspicuous, whether

Far away or intimately close.

Then stand still in your

Newfound unhomely homeland

Of limitless expanse.

Stand still with far and near

In sight; a mind stepping out

Of its state.

Arthur

One time, when I was visiting Samye Ling, I had the honour of meeting this country's first king.

I was staying in the dorm, and they had already warned me beforehand, that they sometimes offer beds for single nights for homeless and wanderers. He showed up just before the soup time; a tall figure of an elderly slender man with ungroomed full beard and grey hair. Clearly knowing his way around, he landed his back pack on the bed.

The way he moved reminded me of a horse, because there was an air of nervousness about it. He blinked his eyes constantly, as if for some reason the light had started to haunt him. Sun burned forehead and cheeks framed piercing blue eyes transfixed to horizon, like there was some kind of trauma just below it; something only he could see glimpses of, without ever being able to fully explain to anyone his predicament.

He told me his annual routine was to travel from northern France all the way up to Scotland and back, getting some money from jobs at construction sites.

He had a son, but they had been 'estranged' for years now. I took that to mean his son had disowned him, but that is just my assumption. It is not an easy task for a foreigner to determine the exact code underneath understated British confiding.

He had no front teeth. At some point some young men with taste for street violence had seen fun in kicking in his teeth, giving him scars which he hid under the beard.

I remember how shocked I was and I remember being ashamed of being shocked. Having had such a sheltered life.

Even now I can still remember the odour of his cheap soap. It lingered in the room days after he had left, like a defiant reminder of the strength of human spirit. Almost like stating, *'I may be homeless, but I have my pride; I am never dirty.'*

Oh, king of Britons, the protector of the weak and the vulnerable, be blessed! I see your suffering when you journeyed through time. How you have been put through the pain of witnessing your subjects' descent to madness. May you find home, solace and peace in your heart and may your children be brought back to the path of justice and charity.

Like Fractals

1

Summer night shows itself in re-occurring
likeness;

from somewhere the smell of ionized air
appears.

Something your nostrils would pick up after a
night of frost.

An hallucination from the opposite end of
the year cycle.

Poplar seeds floating round and landing in
December.

Is this what awaits beyond the perceiver and
the perceived?

2

Inside my brain someone solders a coil for
synesthetic nerve cells.

Rimy fairy rings infest them with their prickly
snow crystals.

Why am I being deceived and who is the
deceiver?

On Our Moonlight Bodies

Our bodies are like vampires, because their pale existences only come alive and animated at night-time. Or like the true splendour of moon gardens; dull and withdrawn at day-time, their whites and greys only become vivid when night falls. As for the potential spectators of these illuminated appearances, what are the chances of finding one in the crowded street? Most are white washed by their sleep and even fewer have sight discerning enough for this. The night owls maybe? Stay alert at times though, when there is a clear night sky with full moon. That's the time you can expect this particular guy to appear – this street-artist of a type. With his black hoody, he looks just like any young graffiti artist, but the truth is: his heart is something exceptional.

The process is always the same.

Picture a scene of this guy

bringing with him

a wet blackboard and

some white chalks.

He then draws inside

the most perfect circle

the most perfect figure

of the most perfect body

of the most perfect deity

and finishes the job

with a tag of his initials

inside the heart-centre.

Very quickly after that

he just vanishes

from the site.

Almost like saying:

'I am not important.

Just keep focused on

the blackboard as it dries.'

So you wait patiently

for the real completion

to begin to unfold...

And then it starts to show.

Breath-taking and

slow paced revealing

of his outlines glorified

in moonlight clarity...

But maybe this is way too far out? To try to fathom such an awe inspiring event? After all, who are we fooling!? It's just a body, completely blind and cut off, using its own limbs to draw a picture of itself. And the truth is, for those eyes that open the next morning this picture is like writing some notes in the middle of the night about a dream we just had, while being half asleep and then slipping seamlessly back to dreamless sleep. So come morning, the ramblings make no sense whatsoever.

Oddity Collision

The early noon is well on its way to become one of the first full-blown sunny midsummer days. With hey and meadows either flowering or starting to flower, and fauna of the insect life at its peak, its chemical cocktail is pungent.

Suddenly we have amongst us this odd man out, who finds the fullness of it all a bit too much. Little by little the overload factors start piling up. There is that smell of cat's pee on the cottage porch. Too much exposure to the sun. A wasp bite. And now a dose of antihistamine. Enough to knock his un-exposed urban body out.

A quick drink to calm his nerves and he is off to dreamland, until the late afternoon dappled shade calls him back from the sofa.

Us happily sunbathing and chatting at the jetty. He takes the stairs down to join us. Unconscious of how sexy he looks with that 'non-hair-product' bed-head of his, we smile at him.

One of us has this five sec delay function in his camera so we decide to take a group photo. And believe it or not, a swallow flying over the jetty photobombs it. Looking at us through the lens like a ghost of a fruit bat from somewhere exotic.

On Far-Offs and Close-Bys

I

Suddenly, from the distance I hear
women chanting a text:

'Calling Guru from
Afar', sounding with it

a vision of a twenty tonne
green-coloured copper bell

levitating above some
mountain village. Then

turning into a thunder-clap,
clear and sound as a bell.

A rumble tearing through
countries and landscapes, till it

eventually arrives at my
ears and hearing.

But what is appearing around me,
I can never be that certain of,

sounding and seeing the way
I am. Could as well be

Taras whispering names
of holy places to my ear, while

I am crammed inside some
early morning dream?

II

Passing probingly through

a series of villages and towns

of continuous no-signal mode

GPS, with unexpected bus stops

turning up in the middle of

somewhere. All orderly lined up,

like meditation cushions in

meticulously arranged rows.

Texting messages from a place

of nowhere particular and

weaving together times

and places over seen

and seeming distances. No

matter the amount of toil,

I never really could tell

apart afar from close-by.

II Eskhaton

On Life Drunkards

To E.D.

It's the middle of the pitch-dark night. A man arrives heavily drunk to a holy place that has neon on the top of its doorway. It spells 'RETREAT' in red over and over again.

Now make no mistake about this, indeed this is a holy facility with a firm set of rules about maintaining its holiness. But I am not so sure about its standards. You know what men are like - good at bending and breaking rules.

Anyway, he wades through the corridors wall-to-wall like it was all just another molten blue sea of alcohol.

He can't remember the number of his room, but that does not stop him from crashing a one. In the dark he then stumbles on a suitcase, falls over it and vomits before passing out.

[57]

Of course he gets thrown out of the place! What did you expect? It's the severest of transgressions.

And what do you think will happen next? Can you think of anything more lenient or more severe? Better or worse?

A man arrives at a retreat so drunk he does not remember it's a retreat.

Containment

The day you came to the island
Was filled with signs of unresolved you.
Arran was hidden behind a wall of water vapour;
An abstract image like Turner's painting
                    Of too distant a promise.
Barely enough to land desert moisture on our lips.

There was also a weirdly oppressive quality
                    Lingering about,
Either suggesting heavy precipitation
Or a thunder storm about to batter the island.
                    Oddly neither happened.

Even a stone could have felt the thirst.

Or at least the pebbles on the paths sure did.

They painted their skins with light.

Reached up to receive the baptising of the rain,

But ultimately remained insatiate.

With only few drops

                    Here and there,

Which gave a speckled look

To their polished surfaces.

At some point the dispense turned into fragility;

Walking on them felt like tiptoeing through

A colony of abandoned and unhatched eggs.

I saw you only once during the day.

I must have walked past your window image,

While carrying a canister of shrine water

To my meditation hut?

You exchanged some words with

Another new face,

Before heading to the dorm.

It was I guess,

An assumption of plenty of artistic freedom;

The image was distorted and peripheral,

Like seen from the bottom of a bottle.

The words fleeting

Like a recording of some

Meaningless daily encounter.

I don't think I would have heard a word

Of what the conversation was about,

Even if I myself were present.

But it sure sounded like what was being served

Was an empty case

Of well-articulated self-delusion.

Yet something managed to escape.
Your blue glance registered and scanned me.
Eyes dead and loveless,

                Soulless like shark's.

An expressionless face of
Convincing enough respectability.
Sleeping around while not a single tear shed.
Denying your fatherhood in all of it.

I took a DNA-sample of it,
With carefully administered pipet drops,
And watched plumes of desolation
Dissolve into holy water.
Yielding a result of a slight change

                Of hue towards blue,

In the way the day was reflected
Through the plastic.

Distraught,
Knowing I will carry in my arms
The memory of that glance for the rest of my life,
I walked back to my hut.

It kept on looking at me,
This oddly silent new born baby;
A container full of tears
You could never cry for yourself,
With its eyes of bottled spring water,
Heavy with thunder light.

                  – Too heavy to carry, actually.

Issue of Address

i

The strangest thing about being stranded here is that I have no idea how long this has been going on. There seems to be no exact dating for its origin. At some point in history Shambhala just vanished from the face of the earth. It's like its leaders looked around and said to themselves. *'The brutes are showing up everywhere and taking over. So let's just go invisible for a while.'* With minds as powerful as these, it only took a single unanimous decision and the whole country went stealth just like that, as if by magic. And yet we are still here, whatever you call us; 'the leftovers', 'the descendants', the few remaining 'head-to-the-clouds poetry enthusiasts'. Once adepts and accomplished ones of holy sites, in which you could witness meaning being born, now landless and wanderers. In a way its disappearance marked the beginning of the era, during which no earthly power has granted the poetic man with domain, he could call his own. What has invaded its place instead, is a manner of speech, which now seems to be prevalent worldwide. It's called 'technically speaking' and for its foul mouth I am part of a group mostly consisting of dregs of society types of individuals, and therefore as an object of measures I present from slight to moderate societal risk. Now it doesn't matter how many times you show your passport to it, or how many times you tell it that you just want to live your mostly lonely and unfulfilling life to its end in peace. Once the mouthpieces of technical terror have the scent of you, and they get their machinery of bullish paperwork mania running, nothing can stop their bloodthirsty manhunt. In recent times countries have become so efficient in this, it's just a matter of time, before I have the boys at MI5 on my trail.

ii

So the 'somewhere-in-the-seeable-future' scenario I am looking at here is as follows: I will be pulled out of my daily life like a tooth and detained for days in some unknown underground facility, so they can satisfy their paperwork feeding frenzy. This amounts to not so amicable process of days of interrogations, which will eventually culminate in my written confession on some tearstained paper. Acknowledging fully that I vow allegiance only to things and have tried to advance their cause with fervour that could almost be described as border lining religious fanaticism; that I recognise myself as a subversive and potentially dangerous societal element and therefore as a registered spy will report to some professional nuisance at the local Job Centre once a fortnight. After the completion of the litany of my stately sins to their liking, they will then quickly typewrite the whole slur and send it back to me. I will be told it is for revision and signature, but it is really all about the most economical action. When it comes to the job of crushing a soul, with people of my ilk nothing does it more elegantly, than to make them see with their own eyes the absolute horror of what they just scribbled in panic. At this stage I am probably ready to meekly sign just about any document. So they will have their papers full of my shaky signatures, all messy with left to right swipes, that trait so typical of effeminate lefties. The process brought to successful end will then be finalised with seals of ink mixed with blood stains; reminiscent of a fairly brutal interrogation technique, too hair raising in nature to be specified in public.

iii

As this is now the projected precipice, Her
Majesty's Royal Mail, those well-meaning idiots,
send me a letter: requesting me to clarify some
issues concerning my address. Now what I know
about the postal services of this country: in regards
of matters of addressing you it is persistent and
cannot be swayed until it gets what it wants. If it is
in your basic nature to be easily shaken, or that
there is natural tendency for flutter, regardless of
any panicky spasms, somehow they know how to
fix the sight to a post, like a missile that sniffs the
poor frightened animal and can hit any shaky
target. My advice to anyone is as follows: when
what they deliver addresses you, just humbly bend
the knee, give paw, catch – whatever, but do it
with well-rehearsed poise. In most cases the best
policy is to totally freeze your movements like a

trained hunting dog. Do not whimper, because then it is likely they will ask more questions. Or if they ring your doorbell, sign the delivery note with a smile, but don't overdo it. This is Royal Mail for goodness sake; not a cult in which you must sing praises to be a good convert. It would be advisable though to spray some perfume to the hall way before you open, just to hide some of the smell of your fear.

iv

'Address? You want to know how to address me? Let me clarify this to your animal instinct... The only thing that separates me from any schizophrenic is the next line I write, which –when you really let it sink in– is just about as fixed as assuming a rat won't gnaw its way through a concrete block if it is certain behind it there is something to eat. It's like Schrödinger's cat-in-the-box, except here of course the cat is a rat, and the box is a concrete block. Now I am sure this more specific characterization will satisfy the 'need-to-know-hunger' of your superiors.'

V

All things considered, I think that went quite well. When he walked back to his car I only noticed a slight shaking in my hand holding the receipt. Did the neighbours notice the incident? Should I be worried about them? I am sure they all think that the reclusive gentleman next door is just a bit jumpy, and there is nothing more to it. And them? Will they come back? Ask more questions? It is likely, when they are so consumed by their world of search and destroy. Who knows how long I can keep doing this, to live as fully as I can, while dodging their perpetual warfare like some almost unrecognizable phantom? What goes for me is the fact dense field sightings are normally not expected in no-man's land; any apparition can pass through its barbed wired terrain without drawing too much attention. That's my hide-away, how I hide myself in plain sight; too outlandish to register, like a mirage of snowy mountaintops appearing between two front lines.

Layers and Reversals

Memorial from Norway's Russian Border Area

House of God.

Open space

full of

       angel light.

Wall,

bottom layer

white limestone

       bathing in daylight,

on the top of which

a thin layer

       of leaf gold

in patched strips.

Hurried swipes of knife cuts

       to right and left;

sweaty labouring,

alarmed looks,

       watch turns.

Bed of earth floor,

peppered with

gold chips and

       mouse droppings.

Puff like

an angel's wing stroke

       at the top of the ceiling.

Men running

in trench coats.

       Stealing gold.

We remain standing.

Stand and linger,

stand and wait.

Death Visualisation

A day in life, which felt like a bad mechanical
toy: a gift far too clunky and oversized to surely
scare small children. It was as if fears of my
mother's renewed cancer merged inseparably
with an image of us in the ward eating my
birthday cake (from the canteen). *'Wonder of still
being around, half a century later.'*

He talked about even distribution of pathogens,
while the fear continued broadcasting in all
directions. Its tasteless, odourless, colourless terror
spreading alongside its weak interactions with
sub-atomic forces of hope. Their quakes so subtle,
the ripples detectable only in the slightest
changes of tones.

He stopped so that I could start to ask troublesome questions like, 'Why the outward spreading movement?', 'It being supra-sensory, what is the receptor for "dread"?', 'Why is the epicentre of the flesh eater forced to reveal itself (in jerks)?' and 'What gradient is used to scan the taste of everything (beyond fear)?'

So we went on with it. A simple procedure of raising the density of the field, which culminates in the final state of koan-receivers. First consuming the bothering questions thoroughly and then slowly dissolving bits of seed syllables to kigu-accent, shaped like a burning question mark and condensed to one taste.

Half-Moon at Holy Isle Boat House

The last quarter by the beach

Weakened and diminished.

The ponies' slow reacting;

Their white trunks

Shying away.

Barely visible

Divergences of grey-white

Deceiving the shine;

Startled faces

Of phantoms

Caught unguarded.

O Noble One,

Is this what it was like?

The night you had your horse saddled,

Rode through the gates,

And tricked the moonlit palace.

Unremembered Epiphany

One Thursday you wake up all clear about it: that today's world is going the wrong way about things, that he has lied to you, and something just doesn't add up. But then you are drawn to the most intense mental image of a wrinkled sheet, still warm with someone's body heat and you start to feel sleepy.

White Noise

Sleep better! Let the
wavelengths gently lull
  you to sleep.
Excerpts of HD WhiteSound™
free download will soothe
  you, while you
browse for other
items that might
  interest you,
like Alfa and
Beta Waves or TV...

...Frequency for bedroom use,

 watching the TV with you

like a white teddy bear.

 ...Sleeping beside you,

giving you good night kisses

of countless childhoods,

or whispering to your ears

 hushed secrets of

lovers – gay or straight.

...Speaking with tongues of men,

World News

like waves of waterfall sounds

packed with inadequate actions

inevitably

cancelling each other out,

like personalized Morse Code

gone mad:

'white, white, white,...'

...The wave of blizzard static of

        your impending death

conveniently zoned out

to embarrassment proof

        mall muzak

of seasons greetings.

Kindly wishing you

        a white noise

Christmas.

...Talking with tongues

  of Angels,

loyal or fallen.

Constantly and in

   all the frequencies,

  like dispersing ripples

of the white noise essence

  in a spectrum of

rainbow noises.

'Gone,

gone,

gone beyond,...'

To the foothills of virtue,

up to the peak.

To space.

To whitest soundwave,

whitest white-water,

whitest deity.

Combustions

I

A divided sensory field of
Late winter plough,
Gently stretching
The rays of sunset
Across the hilly plain.
Casting the last of the light
To the class room wall.

In counter-light
Vapours of steaming manure
Arch towards the icy sky ceiling,
                – Asana like.
Instructing you to rest it
On the tip of your tongue
At the top of the mouth.

II

Have you ever wondered what really went on, when Tilopa was sitting on his pile of rotten fishes, – considering there was also around him the company of maggots swarming underneath him and flies buzzing around? For sure a process of spontaneous combustion was happening all the while, but that is not the point.

Combustion or burning is a chemical process, which is usually very fast and intense. In it all kinds of odd couples form; particles get glued together that under more normal conditions would not bond.

Think of all the elements. They are all children of the first generations of the stars, which during their supernova deaths spew them out into the universe. Iron, silicon, carbon... They were all originally these odd couples that formed under extreme conditions.

Now let's say you are Tilopa's student and you are seeing him meditating on the top of the pile. At some point the slow burning becomes so dense and intense, a mirage appears. First you can see a joyous riot of scales in rainbow colours. Then around Tilopa a dome of light appears, which looks like a finely meshed fishing net made from diamonds.

But what are we to do with these visual signs? Are they representations of the yogi's mind or images from a fly's compound eyes? Or is the mirage a mash-up of the two?

Something was definitely going on with that...

III

Slept too much. Sun-struck and strung up.

Cannot remember anything about yesterday in stereo. Only in mono.

Has no recollections from the beach. Only the bodily feeling of intense heat and behind closed eyelids the impression of colours like orange watercolour dipped to the cup of a black one, with occasional bursts of orange plasm in the mix.

Still feels like about to vomit.

Frazzled by the now already gone head splitting headache.

Deeply troubled by the memory loss.

Gets out of bed.

Slips into sandals.

Ends up nervously pacing around outside the hotel entrance.

Skimming legs like stones across the street into the night, and to the beach. Returns to the 'scene of the crime' as if led by pied piper.

Takes off the sandals and sinks the feet into the sand, still warm from the day's heat.

Somehow the heat felt by the feet fills the gap of lost beach recollections.

Starts to feel more at ease, as if inside his damaged brain there was a switch that needed to be turned on, in order to have the jarring feeling of something set which never arouse go away.

IV

In a watershed moment,
With an act of assault
Lethe force-drinks you
To sip her water.

First lures you in with a
Sparkling net of water ripples
Playing with sewage tunnel roof light,
Then has the story torn into two,
                    – To an arc of
Fading memory, before disappearing
Into the gulping mouth of the night.

Secret Lovers

We were secret lovers.
No-one knew.
Least of all us.

So over the years, we aired it out.
Had our regular meetings
At near-by coffee shops.

Sparred each other through
Those hard to deal with moments
Everyone has.

Same sex, opposite sex;
It doesn't matter.
Intimacy condensed itself to words.

It did not tarnish itself
With conquests and disasters
Of our sexual histories,

Declining from enthusiasm to

Bittersweet disappointment,

But stayed within the confines of our hearts.

Lasting and noble, it earned its crown:

Love so deep, it came to life, thrived and died

Covered by the shroud of the unsaid.

The Legend of Saint Molaises Cave

It is told that the saint's last winter in Holy Isle was very difficult, with winds strong and chilly lasting for weeks. He also suffered from a disease of unknown origin. Unable to find its cause and its cure, and when the fever kept on staying high night after night, he grew weaker each day.

That evening, knowing another night of torment with delirium and nightmares would wait for him, he was finally ready to accept his demise. Certain this was his last night on earth, in desperate prayers he asked God's mercy to save his still young life or if he would deem better otherwise, save his soul.

After his prayers he noticed a curious thing, – something that had never crossed his mind before, though he had been living in his cave for so long. Its layout was shaped like a fish.

Right that very moment, almost as if by invitation, a man clothed in light appeared. He gently laid his hand on Saint Molaises chest and said God had sent him to deliver a message. To the saint's surprise the angel then started chastising him:

'Indeed, you are no better than what Jonah was! You are more concerned about proving yourself right than doing God's work. Why are you still troubled by such things? In your cave aren't you already inside the fish, you who already are its nourishment?'

'Consider also the fishes, blessed by The Son. It took only a single day for them to become chosen for Christendom's banquet. They lost their lives for many. Yet before that they knew neither God's ways nor his plans. Why would your origin be less humble?'

'You are already in God's fishing net and you will provide for many. You think yourself weak and poorly, yet your life is being prepared to be *sacrificed for Christendom. For so it shall be: you will be fishes and loaves for many.'*

The angel then went on to explain it is God's will he should procrastinate no more and that he should start laying out plans to see Pontiff already tomorrow. He was also told to study in his heart a part of God's word so he could share the result of his contemplation with Pontiff and his court.

Finally he was assured not to worry. His ailment was in the Almighty's hands and he should get some rest. After this the angel's light faded into the night.

Next morning the fever was gone. So sudden was its disappearance, the saint was convinced the angel had taken it with him. Filled in his heart with relief, joy and gratitude, in his prayers he thanked the Lord for his plan to offer his life for Christendom. He also thanked his little island for giving him a cave in the shape of a fish. Then like he was told to do, he started drawing plans for his journey.

Mind Rorschach

In Loving Memory of Chöje Akong Tulku Rinpoche

Rinpoche's dead

And I am stuffing pizza and candy

To the back pockets of my numb mind,

Filling the blanks and dark corners

In a world that has run hot,

Transfixed and dried.

I see a picture of three men

Up on the hillside

With wind caressing grasses.

Like it all was just him,

Everywhere.

But they would not notice.

Instead a stern look at each other

Before descending.

One man for each:

Done deal,

Premeditated, planned.

Scenes of brother against brother,

World against itself.

And upon the plain of

This briefest battle

A wind that touches

The curl of your hair.

I can't –

There's tears on my pizza.

I won't –

That looks like a–

Self Portraits

1

I am zigzag the stripes;
The colours yellow, black and white.
Like rushes behind rushes,
They all are bending and in motion.

Inside a random heap of shapes
I am a 3D-illusion about a forest.
An alarming picture
Only a short-sighted can see.

You don't recognize me
In everything you see.
You can't see me coming,
Until it is too late.

In a way I am the ultimate trickster.

2

Mine are the sounds of

Dry leaves swirling and

The warning signals spreading

Across the canopy.

I'm closing in,

When there is a sudden sound

Of a twig breaking,

Or deers charging.

I am the dry monsoon forest.

I am the tiger.

I am the tiger in the forest.

I am the tiger-forest.

Your senses are no match to me.

3

I ambush you
In the scattered rhythms of
Grasshoppers' chirp playing with
Shade and sunlight.

I am just one leap.
A painful sting in your neck
And a snapping sound
Of it breaking.

I am the patient wait
Of your grasping turning feeble.
I am your fading heart pounding.
I am your heart.

I am Samsara.

Autumn Mandala

It's hard to believe I lived in this city all those years. It was more of a chaotic beast then.

The more you see the more it feels like a complete stranger; I turn left, I turn right, but cannot seem to find any familiar looking street view.

If someone right now were to give directions from the balcony of the City Hall, I would not be addressed.

They even changed its name. It is now called the City of Humanity.

Poste restante, I now live from one day to the next with the local birds.

Save occasional attempts to cling to what can be shown and contrivance and boredom, which follow them like elongated shadows, all of us are

[104]

past mating season, at a loss and with nothing to sing for.

It's like uttering my name with a big sigh. Blowing away with that outbreath all the landmarks of personal history.

Cutting late summer roses in a vase. Planted once with love, but now I guess, forgotten to a neglected corner, where no-one comes to marvel at them.

While it becomes harder and harder to remember the stem of it, let alone its genealogy and family name, I keep in mind whatever its promise, it always comes with thorns.

Fragrance, shy like the glance of young lady Di. My imaginary cultivar, I think I will call you 'Desire'.

Fascinated by *memento mori* of flowers withering. For some reason I find the random groupings of petals spread over the tablecloth enjoyable.

Descriptions are becoming increasingly transient by day. Changing colour, first from distinct pink to a fading one and then right at the end – before the petals start to fall, becoming almost completely white.

Is its essence pink, pale pink or white? You tell me.

Effaced of any self-consciousness, it opens out from the centre.

Not coy at all in its allure. It's like watching in silence someone undressing, who has never learned how to be ashamed of his body.

A murmur of lower powers, one caused by the undeniably shortening days, hiding in the background noise.

Seventeen gestures. More telling about what will be left of me than any detail of life history ever could.

Eskhaton

Your dreams are seamless at the end of it all.
And women as always, will outlive men
To actually take notice. *'Has Jesus come yet?'*
'Everything is fine, Granny. Go back to sleep.'
It will be like one big dream.

      ·   Death will come tonight.

Under electric light, by the kitchen table,

They –the wombs of storytelling,

Will talk about the ebbs and flows of

The life we shared. And they will be wondering

What they could tell to their children

And grand-children.

But there are no words.

So powerful is the light that shines
On our hardships and misfortunes,
The ink becomes blindingly bright.
And as the mystery illuminates
Every word, every sentence,
Every page, you are left
But wondering: Did it really start
At some point? Are you sure
It will have an end?

Maybe that's it?
That the last lines are only for poets.

Printed in Great Britain
by Amazon